American Government

Supreme Court

by Connor Stratton

FOCUS READERS®
PIONEER

www.focusreaders.com

Copyright © 2024 by Focus Readers®, Lake Elmo, MN 55042. All rights reserved. No part of this book may be reproduced or utilized in any form or by any means without written permission from the publisher.

Focus Readers is distributed by North Star Editions:
sales@northstareditions.com | 888-417-0195

Produced for Focus Readers by Red Line Editorial.

Photographs ©: Shutterstock Images, cover, 1, 12, 17; Fred Schilling/US Supreme Court, 4; Red Line Editorial, 7; Franz Jantzen/US Supreme Court, 8; Andrew Harnik/AP Images, 11; Steve Petteway/US Supreme Court, 15, 21; Eric Lee/Pool via CNP/picture alliance/Consolidated News Photos/Newscom, 18

Library of Congress Cataloging-in-Publication Data
Names: Stratton, Connor, author.
Title: Supreme Court / Connor Stratton.
Description: Lake Elmo : Focus Readers, 2023. | Series: American government | Includes index. | Audience: Grades 2-3
Identifiers: LCCN 2023002927 (print) | LCCN 2023002928 (ebook) | ISBN 9781637395943 (hardcover) | ISBN 9781637396513 (paperback) | ISBN 9781637397640 (pdf) | ISBN 9781637397084 (ebook)
Subjects: LCSH: United States. Supreme Court--Juvenile literature. | Constitutional law--United States--Juvenile literature. | Judicial process--United States--Juvenile literature.
Classification: LCC KF8742 .S77 2023 (print) | LCC KF8742 (ebook) | DDC 347.73/26--dc23/eng/20230403
LC record available at https://lccn.loc.gov/2023002927
LC ebook record available at https://lccn.loc.gov/2023002928

Printed in the United States of America
Mankato, MN
082023

About the Author

Connor Stratton writes and edits nonfiction children's books. He lives in Minnesota.

Table of Contents

CHAPTER 1
The Highest Court 5

CHAPTER 2
Becoming a Justice 9

CHAPTER 3
Taking Cases 13

The Constitution 16

CHAPTER 4
The Law of the Land 19

Focus on the Supreme Court • 22
Glossary • 23
To Learn More • 24
Index • 24

Chapter 1

The Highest Court

The Supreme Court leads one part of the US **government**. This part is called the judicial branch. The court has nine **justices**. They say what laws mean.

Judges run lower courts. They make **rulings**. But people can **appeal**. Then a higher court takes the **case**. It makes a ruling. People can appeal again. The case can reach the Supreme Court. It is the highest US court.

Did You Know? States have their own courts. Their cases can go to the Supreme Court, too.

US Court System

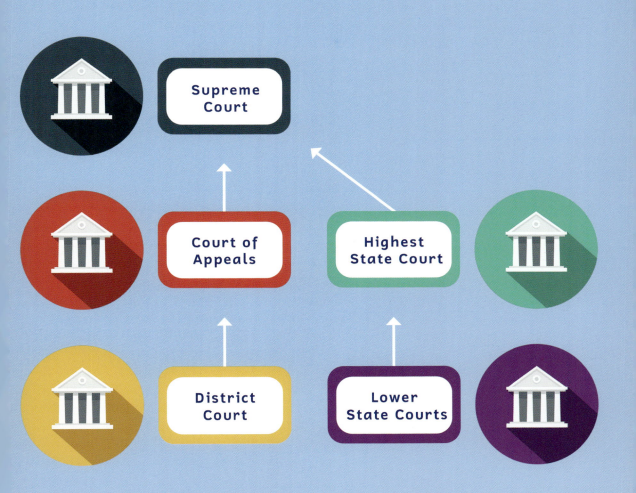

Chapter 2

Becoming a Justice

Supreme Court justices are trained in the law. Most justices went to law school. Many of them worked as judges. Some taught. Others were lawyers. Lawyers help others with the law.

Sometimes the court has an opening. Then the **president** picks a justice. That person goes to the **Senate**. Lawmakers ask questions. Then they vote. More than half must vote yes. Then that person can be a justice.

Did You Know? Justices can serve for life. But some stop working before they die.

11

Chapter 3

Taking Cases

Many appeals reach the Supreme Court. But the court takes just a few. It chooses not to rule on most appeals. Those cases stay with the lower court. Its rulings are then final.

Each case has two sides. Both sides have lawyers. They say why their side is right. Justices listen to both sides. They ask questions. Then they talk with one another.

Did You Know? The Supreme Court gets thousands of appeals every year. It takes fewer than 200.

A Closer Look

The Constitution

The United States has a **Constitution**. The country has used it since 1789. It explains important beliefs. It explains important laws, too. The **document** helps the Supreme Court. The court uses it to check laws. All laws must follow it.

We the People
domestic Tranquility, provide for the comm
our Posterity, do ordain and establish this Co
Article. I
Section. 1. All legislative Powers herein granted shall be vested in a Congress of the United States, which shall co
Section. 2. The House of Representatives shall be composed of Members chosen every second Year by the People

Chapter 4

The Law of the Land

The Supreme Court thinks about cases. The court considers many things. It looks to the Constitution. It looks to lower courts. The court also looks to past rulings.

Justices talk to one another. They talk about each side. More than half must agree. Then the court rules. Each ruling matters. No one may appeal it. All courts must follow it.

Did You Know? The court's rulings have a name. They are called opinions.

FOCUS ON
The Supreme Court

Write your answers on a separate piece of paper.

1. Write a few sentences describing how cases reach the Supreme Court.

2. Would you want to meet a Supreme Court justice? Why or why not?

3. How long do justices serve on the Supreme Court?
- **A.** for nine years
- **B.** for 16 years
- **C.** for life

4. What happens if a lower court disagrees with a Supreme Court ruling?
- **A.** It can appeal the ruling.
- **B.** It can ignore the ruling.
- **C.** It must follow the ruling.

Answer key on page 24.

Glossary

appeal
To ask a higher court to review a case.

case
A problem people take to court for a decision on it.

Constitution
The document that lays out the basic beliefs and laws of the United States.

document
A record of something, such as an image, film, or writing.

government
The people and groups that run a city, state, tribe, or country.

justices
People who decide cases in courts of law.

president
The leader of the United States.

rulings
Decisions on cases.

Senate
One part of Congress. Congress is the part of the US government that makes laws.

To Learn More

BOOKS

Kortuem, Amy. *The U.S. Supreme Court*. North Mankato, MN: Capstone Press, 2020.

Smith-Llera, Danielle. *Exploring the Judicial Branch*. Minneapolis: Lerner Publications, 2020.

NOTE TO EDUCATORS

Visit **www.focusreaders.com** to find lesson plans, activities, links, and other resources related to this title.

Index

A
appeals, 6–7, 13–14, 20

C
Constitution, 16, 19

L
lawyers, 9, 14

O
opinions, 20

Answer Key: 1. Answers will vary; 2. Answers will vary; 3. C; 4. C